The Random Rhymes
of
Inspiration

Jennifer Miller

WestBow
PRESS
A DIVISION OF THOMAS NELSON

ISBN: 978-1-4497-5825-7 (sc)

Library of Congress Control Number: 2012911631

WestBow Press books may be ordered through booksellers or by contacting:

WestBow Press
A Division of Thomas Nelson
1663 Liberty Drive
Bloomington, IN 47403
www.westbowpress.com
1-(866) 928-1240

Printed in the United States of America

WestBow Press rev. date: 07/13/2012

INTRODUCTION

Let it be said of us that we walk down the
path that leads to life, not looking back or from
side to side. This path we're on were not alone, we
all go through trials, temptations and pain. This
book is full of stories that are not the same.

I wrote this book of Rhyme and Reason to inspire
you all with inspiration, to let you know that there is a
god who has the power to break your chains, heal your
pains, heal your scars and you'll never be the same.

He is a god without tainted lips, he doesn't speak
lies or let you slip, he loves you more than you will
know, just open the door and you'll be restored.

ACKNOWLEDGMENTS

I would first of all like to say thank you to my husband Mark for playing a huge role in helping me move forward in my walk with the Lord, and for showing me that a life without Christ is useless.

I would also like to thank my four children for inspiring me to write stories. My oldest son Luke is 19 years old, Tiffany age 17 is my second oldest, third in line is Shayla who is 11, whom also helped write the contents page for me, and then my youngest son Isaiah is 8.

I would also like to thank my church family for all the prayers and opportunities to get connected in a church, and to grow in a place where I feel the Lord has planted me, so that I may grow in my faith, and be nourished. So I say, Thank you Orchardville Community Church.

Last but not least, I would like to thank God who has brought me out of darkness and into his light, for setting my feet on a solid foundation, for guiding me and leading me and teaching me to follow him.

CONTENTS

I am a small town girl, born and raised in Southern Illinois; I grew up in a small town of Orchardville, It's surrounded now by Amish horses and buggies.

Life as a teen was almost unbearable with violence and abuse taken a toll on family life. I had a dream within my heart of becoming a radio dj, making my own recordings and interviewing random people, but quickly giving up on that dream of ever becoming one, not realizing the dream that was being birthed inside me was really a desire to speak and to tell my stories for those who love to hear.

I left home at the age of 18, then marrying my high school sweetheart Mark at the age of 19. Our family then began to grow, and we now have four kids: Luke, Tiffany, Shayla and Isaiah, all ranging from 19 to 8.

Several years later I was introduced to the savior of my soul, and from that day forward my life has changed dramatically, trying to find my purpose in life, walking now by faith and not by sight. Feeling the need to begin college and to write a book, not knowing where this book will take me, but now leaving it in the hands of the great I AM. My dream began one day as my son Luke was out in the shed looking for something to work on. I decided I would go out and visit with him, I noticed four boxes of books that he had brought home one day from work. He left them laying on the floor, my curiosity got the best of me and I began to take the books out one by one and laid them on the floor until I ran across one book that caught my attention. It was a book on how to be a writer. I opened the book and began to read it.

I then began to pray for Gods will and direction in my life. A few days later as I was taking a shower I began to pray again for the same thing and the title to my first story came to me, Jeanie in a Bottle, then the Holy Spirit began to speak to me. I quickly went and got the computer and placed it on the table, and thought I need my bible just in case I need to look something up. I stuck my hand in a random place and flung the book open, to the very page the Holy Spirit had spoken to me. Shocked and trembling I began to write my first story, it was written about my grandmother Jean and the life she chose to live.

After writing a few more stories I then began some basic college studies and I laid my book aside. One early morning before my eyes were awakened, I heard the voice of the Lord say to me that first things are first. It was one of my pastor's sermons, surprised and awake; I came down the stairs and looked up my pastor's sermon online and found that very one, as I began to watch, it was then that I realized God was telling me to get back to writing my book.

That very evening my daughter Tiffany wanted to take a four-wheeler ride down to low-water Bridge, a road less traveled, but because it was cold and breezy I really didn't want to go, but she talked me into going. We got down to low-water bridge and seen that it was flooded over so we turned around and drove up the embankment and there in the weeds under a bush was a wet book in fairly good condition with the cover rolled back and on the top page I noticed it was a writing book, I said to my daughter grab that book! As she handed the book to me I realized it was a college addition. I looked at my daughter and she looked at me, and I said I think God is telling me to get back to writing, she said "*yes mom,*

I think your right," I took the book home and dried the pages and began to read and study this book on my own, and eventually ended up taking a college class on English Writing and it has helped my dramatically. This writing book has been the bases and structure for my book, and has given me a great opportunity to share my dream.

Jeanie in a Bottle

There was an old woman who lived in the sticks she loved being a hermit; it gave her quite a kick, living a life of lonesome way, never to retrieve the light of day. Showers by water-hoses, buckets of toilets, poodles named peppy who was frightened half to death. She screamed at her neighbors and greased their knobs she peaked out the windows and watched them sob. Then one day as her life began to fail, she ended up in a nursing home and then raised hell.

The nurses didn't like her and stole her treats, wouldn't give her a bath or change her sheets. I came to see her and shared a hug; she turned her head and then just shrugged. *"Why does my life have to be this way? My eyes are blind, and my teeth have fallen out, what is there left but an awfully sad life, never to walk again and only a breath."* Then one day as she became very ill, my mother and I wheeled her through the E.R room, she cried out loud *"which way, which way, which way do I go, someone help me if you know, is it left? Is it right? I cannot tell, the path is dark and I'm scared as hell."*

She's now lying on a bed slipping in and out of consciousness, I'm sending up prayers as quickly as possible, and then across the room a voice calls out, *"I am a Christian woman and that's what I'm about!"* I looked to see who was behind the voice, a very little woman in a bed far away looks right at me as if to say, yes you, I'm talking to you. I looked around and all I could see was that every head was bowed to the knee.

I'm not sure as what to say, so I lift my thumb high in the air and then I said praise the lord someone cares. As her day got weaker and her hours got shorter, the preacher came in to share the father, he opened up the bible and began to read, filling our hearts with hope and peace, waiting to see how long she would last, only an hour that would pass, her last breath came as we stood by her side, as she passed from this life while we all said goodbye.

The life of this old woman was built on selfishness and greed, she never liked people but always wanted to be free, she lived in the woods near a lake as you see, she fished a lot and caught her own bait, and she went to town once a week with a truck full of jugs and a frown on her face, her life was a mess and full of disgrace. She enjoyed stealing from her neighbors and greasing their knobs, it always made her laugh to see someone cry, but little did she know about the days to come, as her body grew weak and her head just hung, her eyes grew faint and wouldn't respond.

Her days in the nursing home took a toll on her life, she became very angry, sad and depressed, and she screamed at the nurses and yelled at the cooks, *"give me my glasses so I can have a look!"* She never combed her hair or let anyone touch her, I wondered why her life was in complete disaster, she bottled up her heart and never let it out, until one day as her days became hours, a preacher came in to read from the bible, he began to read the from the book of Romans, and asked, *"Jeanie can you pray? Repeat after me,"* the room filled with joy and my heart filled with peace, Jeanie in the Bottle has now been set free.

The Tree and It's Fruit

I'm taking trash to the dumpster, yes indeed, long behold there is an apple tree, lying to the side with a cut at the base, surrounded by stink, O' what a waste. Not sure as to how it got in this place, as I look real close I notice one thing. The tree has apples, and the leaves are burnt, uprooted and dragged and left in the dirt, one light of a match and it will all be gone, never again will the tree bear fruit, but will only leave behind, fertilized dirt.

Escaping the Flame

Butch was a mailman highly esteemed, he lived
to bring mail to each family you see, he put the
pedal to the metal and sped away, hoping to make
his rounds before the sunset that day. For years and
years he carried the mail, sending out Christmas cards
and buckets of cheer, he was the nicest man anyone
could know until one day our mail didn't show.

No one knew as to why he didn't come, but then
as time passed we all just gasped, Butches car was hit
by a train, caught on fire and blew up in a flame, his
life then ended and no mail to be seen, until two days
later it was retrieved, as I opened the box and the smoke
rolled out, my eyes filled with tears and my heart just
sunk. Butch will be remembered by the life that he lived,
filled with commitment and the duty that was his.

THE MYSTERY OF THE MISSING BAG

Lonnie was a man that was nice and sweet, he
never made you mad or frowned at your feet, he
always had a smile and was ready to greet, if he wasn't
at one door he'd be at the other, greeting the people
as they went through the foyer. With a shiny bald
head and big white teeth, he never had anything
bad to say about the people he'd meet. He loved to
give doughnuts as a special treat, the bag he gave me
someone must of eat, never did I see them, no not one.

The next Sunday came and he asked with a smile,
"Were the doughnuts good?" My heart began to panic and
my palms began to sweat, with my head hung low, I
said, well I don't really know, the doughnuts you gave
me vanished without a trace. I never got home with them
and they never got ate. With a serious look upon his face,
his mouth dropped open and fell to the ground, stunned
that the doughnuts had never been found. Where did
they go? I do not know. When the shock wore off, he said
with a smile, "don't worry honey, I'll see you tomorrow.

Rehab Dave

As we went to a rehab center one day, to see a man named Ed, the man in the bed to his left you see was very lonely as he could be, not sure as to why he was staring at me, so I went on over to take a look, then he opened up his mouth and then he spoke, never will I forget what he said that day. *"My life is almost over, my body is in pain, my legs won't move and I've lived a life of shame, I'm filled with addictions that I can't break away. God, will you help me, I need someone to pray, I have no family and I'm wasting away. I've been on this bed for weeks on end waiting for a Chaplin who never came in." "How long will I be here, how long will I last, then you walked in and I knew in a flash, you were the one that I've been waiting on."* With Joy by my side we took hold of his hands, as our prayer filled the room and the holy spirit moved, Dave's hands began to shake and his eyes filled with tears, never in his life has he known such love, never will we forget what happened from above, as I looked back at Dave and waved farewell, he sat there in shock as his tears still fell. That was the last time I seen his face, I bet he'll be at the pearly gates.

The Good Samaritan

There was an old man who lived out back, on the break of day he would get away on his bike he would go, flying down hills and feeling the breeze, with the wind at his front and the wind at his back, he never was sure of where he was at, passing the trees as he wobbled about with an orange reflector in a place unseen, dropping his bike off amongst the weeds.

Where he was going nobody did know, then one day as I was on my way beside an old abandoned school, with its walls fallen down and the roof caved in, there in the distance what seemed to be, was the old man beside the apple tree, as I pulled up and began to speak, he pulled his bike up out of the weeds.

He said *"what are you doing here following me? Are you my nurse I can't really see,"* no sir I said, it's only me, I was out for a ride and seen you ahead, and thought to myself I'm glad he's not dead.

THE LIPS OF AN ANGEL

Standing in the night with the light of the moon,
behind an old building and a building that was
new, with a girl to my right and a girl to my left,
holding hands in a circle and praying for the best,
thinking were alone and no one to disturb, as our
prayers are being lifted I know were being heard.

When all of the sudden high in the sky a voice started
singing as I opened my eyes, looking above with nothing
to see wondering if I'm the only one who hears this
mysterious thing. I close my eyes and continue to pray,
it was the sweetest moment in history. To my surprise
the girls did say they heard some singing far away.

Not a moment later as we opened our eyes, there
before us was a great surprise, standing on the building in
the leaves of the tree, hiding in the branches but visible to
me was a figure of a boy that only we could see, scared and
trembling and unable to move, we called out to the boy on
the roof, he gave no answer, we were afraid to move close.

Not sure of who it might be, we called out again and
he answered our plea, *"yes I was singing when I heard you
pray, my heart filled with joy and I began to give praise,
singing Lips of an Angel as I stood on the peak, lifting up
praises as you speak."* to my surprise I recognized the boy
who was just inside, somehow he slipped out without
a trace and climbed up in this inconspicuous place.

Jennifer Miller

THE UNSEEN GUEST

Cleaning away in the kitchen one day making it spick and span, cranking the music up to a 10 and feeling the beat within, as my feet start to move and I'm dancing in groove singing as loud as I could, my son walks in and says, *"someone is looking in."* I see a man with a smirkey grin, and I said to the lord dig me a hole for now I am jumping in, my heart skipped a beat and I said real sweet, I am not letting him in.

As I tried to hide but swallowed my pride, the lord said, *"let him in,"* as I walked to the door and opened it up he stood there with a big grin. I asked the lord why he was there and watched me unaware, the lord replied, *"his spirit was dry and needed to cry until he seen you dance, his heart filled with joy and then was refreshed and then he was able to laugh."*

Sam I Am

Tiff and I spent the night in the ER room, waiting
on Doctor Corky to come in soon, it took an hour or
so it seemed, then in stepped a man who looked oddly
keen, he had the nicest voice and spoke soft hearted, he
said. *"My mane is Sam and I will get your IV started"*

Sam just smiled and made preparations, he took the
needle and shot the light and showered the room and
gave us quite a sight. We started to laugh as Sam was
quite funny, as British man Sam finished what he was
doing, he packed up his cart and walked towards the
door, when I looked at his face, Sam giggled some more.

THE CROSS WILL LEAD ME HOME

Driving through the dead of the night, not a soul that was in sight, I'm taking a trip to an unknown place, trying to remember what marked this place. Two hours out as the sun is rising, there in the distance at the peak of the hill was the largest cross I have ever seen. With seats around so all could see the remarkable beauty of this glowing thing.

Six hours out as I'm in a strange land, with corn fields and fodder stalks all around, not very comfortable about this place that I'm in. Desolate and dry and no one around, ready to return to the place I began. Finally at last my time was done; I'm now on the road that returns to home.

Driving by faith is the way to go, as I'm blaring the radio and singing along, praying I take the right road home. Four hours out and I come to a fork, not sure of which way I'm suppose to look, left or right or straight through the middle, my heart is now pounding and my legs start to sweat, not sure of where I am going to end up.

There in the distance as I topped the hill the glorious cross with a glow so bright, filled my heart with such delight, I knew at last I was almost home. I'm glad this trip has come to an end. The cross of Christ is where I began.

Freedom Without – Freedom Within

Troubled family troubled life, beatings in the morning beatings at night, O' how I wish there was peace from within, outwardly living but inwardly dying, unable to break away, with a chain on my hand and a chain on my foot, I wonder what will be the outlook. Nobody cares; I'm all alone, with bruises on my head and bruises on my arms, no broken bones but only scars. Scars that fester, scars that heal, is this a dream or is it real. I want to get out but where do I go, someone tell me if you know.

Now lying on a bed being beat in the head, throwing up nonstop till I'm almost dead, unable to move, as weak as could be, what in the world is happening to me. My stomach is burning, my chest is on fire, I think that my life is almost over, unaware if I will get help, my mother and brother come and pick me up, I can't raise my head or move a muscle, they drag me to the car as my feet stir the dust. Will I ever forgive? Will I ever trust? That is a story that is a must. I choose to forgive and not hold a grudge, because I have been forgiven, and that I can trust.

Jennifer Miller

The Number of the Beast

The birth of a child, the unspoken words, numbers and letters are all unheard, 6 lbs and 6 oz is what she was, unable to believe at what time she had come. The day or the hour how could we know, simply 6:30 was when she was born. The birth daddy showed and tried to get in, but he had no right after what he did.

He was a drug addict who lived on the streets, spreading unfaithfulness for people's feet, luring them in and planting his seeds, not caring who his next victim might be. He's like a breast that runs about, hiding in places and scouting them out, pulling them in with his smooth speech, "Come, come," he cries in the street, while placing a net for the simple and weak, little does he know that the path he is on will come to an end in the pits of hell.

LOVE OF THE FATHER

Red balloons and a teddy bear, a little girl with curly hair, walking around in a public square, with a man who didn't care, with one string she was tied to a cart, little did she know the with one whisper the man untied her and then just left her, she wandered around for half an hour, crying out loud for someone to find her, never was he seen again never was he found.

The girl was found by a Wal-Mart worker, who then began to try to help her. The girl chewed her fingers and cuddled her bear, hoping someday she would be found, by a special someone who really loved her. Love is what she wanted; love is what she needed, waiting for a father who would never leave her. Christ is his name he is always the same, yesterday, today and forever.

Jennifer Miller

HEAVENS REIGN

I'm out on the town as I'm driving along, I'm looking
around and this is what I saw: Two people are lost and
can't find their cars, one's smoking a doo-be at the
tire store, three are crippled and can't get to the door,
ones leaning against the building as if he had no cares,
one's standing by the road with his thumb in the air.

As I continue to drive with the wind in my hair,
something special blows through the air, it begins to rain
pink flowers and the smell of perfume, and showers my
van as I'm driving through, ending this trip on a happy
note, I'm singing my heart out and that's all she wrote.

THESE FOUR WALLS

Beatings within the walls, the screaming fits, will this end or will this stick, there's nothing I can do, I'm only a kid, trying to hid from the things I did, was it me or was it him, I'm so confused and mislead, is there freedom or a deadly end, with a punch in the mouth and swelled up lips. Thank god it's the weekend so I can heal up.

Maybe no one will notice my bruised up arms, and my legs are scratched with chain marks. The lightning strikes, the thunder sounds he's now been hit by a fiery flame, flying now at the speed of sound, he is now lying on the ground, the rooms on fire and my ears are deaf, not sure what happed but scared to death.

The fires now out as I'm hiding beneath the sheets; I'm now crying myself to sleep. The days to come how could I have known, my arms are weak and I'm barley holding on, I find a bible and pick it up, only to find I had no luck, I never understood so I laid it down, only to find it had a gravitational pull. I couldn't let go no matter how hard I tried.

There was an emptiness that was inside, all that I know is I'm living in hell, this has to end but I don't know how, nobody will help me and I'm hell bound, feeling trapped within these four walls, will this end or will I be scared. This is not the life I wanted to live, if only there was safety from within.

The clock is ticking and I'm leaving home, I'm going to a place that is not my own, I have my own room and a dresser drawer, this is much better than it was before, no more beatings or crying on the floor, no more bruises or bangs on the door, I'm now surrounded by honey bees, the hand of God has set me free, he has taken my shame, and picked me up out of the miry clay, he has set my feet on solid ground, and now my life has turned around.

You Have Worth

In the expanse of the sky, the moon shines bright,
a new day will dawn at just the right time. Does
anyone know what the day will bring, only God
in heaven who is the king. Some will have peace,
some live in shame, some will be persecuted because
of his name, some will be insulted and left with
pain, people will say you're not worth anything.

Is that really the truth, or have they spoken in vain?
God has a purpose and a plan for your life, he's given you
a ring like a beautiful bride, he's colored your life like a
painted sky, with glorious riches down deep in the soul,
how in the world could others know, your beauty shines
like a rainbow bent on a beam, glowing with brilliant
colors displayed for all to see, who then has noticed, who
then has seen, the remarkable beauty of the enter me.

TRIVIA

He stands on a podium with a tail down his back, he leads with a stick, and doesn't look back, he sways to the music and doesn't miss a beat, pounding the air with his hands and his feet and banging his head unto the beat, he raises up high and bends down low this has now become an unbelievable show, he has now taken on the magnetic flow, as the people then stand to applaud what they see, he then turns around with his hands on his knees and gives the audience what they've been waiting to see.

Question # 1: Who is the story talking about?

    A. Clown

    B. Conductor

    C. Singer

Question # 2: What was the audience waiting to see?

    A. Stunt

    B. Wave

    C. Bow

Answers:

Question # 1: B

Question # 2: C

FAME

Lying on a blanket under the moonlit sky, watching the clouds as they ripple by, dreaming someday that I'll spread my wings and fly somewhere I've never been, something tells me the time is close, the clock is ticking for a time unknown. The sound the lights are shining bright, the base the curl the purple liner, I'm not sure all this really matters. From one to ten, I've left a trail, that reveals to everyone where I've been.

As the oil flows down and anoints my head, the lady then says it's time to begin, with a mic in my hand, my mouth opens up, words begin spewing like a fire from the brook, flowing through the air gliding on a current, the crowd goes wild at that very moment, chanting my name to levels unheard, I now hear the voice of a multitude, as I stand in awe of Gods amazing grace, reality has now hit me in the face, that God has put me in this place.

Jennifer Miller

The Big Slip Up

Flying free and fast as can be the little bird is watching me, with a ruby red throat and a shiny green back, he drinks the drink and then comes back, he grasps his feet around the perch until he slips and then gets hurt, he's now face down, caught by his neck, his heart is pounding out of his chest, a boy walks by and see's his distress, breaks him free and gives him rest.

Sometimes in life we may mess up, were going along good and then slip up. We find ourselves ensnared by sin and wonder how we got pulled in. God hears our distress and knows where we've been, but remember nothing is too hard for him, if we cry out, he is faithful, he will break the chains and calm our hearts, and give us rest in his arms.

The Canoe Trip

Were cruising down stream in a canoe, with sixteen
people and one that was new, everything was going
smooth until we went around a corner and one flipped
his canoe, all his stuff went floating down stream, until
we caught it and put it back in. Moving along as the
current flows, another canoe spins out of control.

It flips upside down as the two fall out. They
go under the water and then pop up. They cry for
help to a passerby, who then jumps in and swims to
their side. As the sun goes down, we set up camp
everything we have is now all wet, sitting around
a fire as we sing camp songs, eating gritty burgers
that fell in the sand, now it is time to go to bed.

Day two were off to a start, racing down river and
then get caught, thunder and lightning is crashing
about, and we head for cover upon a sandbar. Josh
whips up a shelter with sticks and a tarp, were huddling
together just to keep warm, the storm lets up and we
head out again, only this time we come to the end.

Hung by a Thread

A man that's caught between life and death, who's
straddling the fence, he wants to live in paradise but
he's hanging by a thread, he thinks there is no hope to
spare, so he beats his wife in the head, he runs to hide
from the things he's done and climbs upon a ladder. He
takes his life in his hands and hangs himself to death,
the narrow road that leads to life he did not abide, if
only he would have given, all of his life to Christ.

We Never Walk Alone

Standing in the road with one flat tire, wondering
what I should do, as I look to the north upon the
third hill, thinking about walking over, my mind
goes back unto my past at a time when I was younger,
I cannot go, I will not go the life that is now over, I
wiped the dust off of my feet a left that life behind.

In an instant I am now surrounded by a swarm
of honey bees, eight or nine I do believe that came
unto my aid. A smooth hand to release the spare
and two that brought the help, one with strength
to break the bolts and set the tire free, one to
pick an orange flower and handed it to me.

Love and comfort did I feel as I did not
stand alone, I now have a family that servers
the Lord, and I will never walk alone.

THE DAY WE HAD NO LUCK

Heading out to the beach one day ready to ride the boat, something tells me this is the day we will not have any luck, the call comes in my sisters stranded and needs a helping hand, were on our way were driving fast and then another call, my other half has blown a hose and sitting on the road. We pick up parts were on our way and come to the interstate, there in the grass shaded by trees under a pink umbrella, is my sister and her family waiting for my arrival, we load them in and all their stuff and now were off again.

A few miles up unto my left is my other half, we pulled to the shoulder two teens jump out and then they ran on over. We then take off and arrive at the beach a little late for dinner, we change our clothes and head to the shore and then a storm blows over, waves are crashing over the boat until it begins to sink, we grab the cooler and a cup and began to scoop it out, finally at last the boat starts up and they go to put it up, we all decide this is the day that we did not have any luck.

Not a One Way Street

There once was a man who lived alone, who would
sit upon his bed, he wondered why he had no friends
and lived his life in dread. Every morning he would
feed his dog hotdogs and bologna, and wondered
why no one would stop to see how he was doing.

Then one day I went to see the man on lonely lane,
there upon the big oak tree in view for all to see, along
the two lane highway was the words *"No Trespassing"* I
drove on up and honked my horn until he hobbled out, he
asked me why no one comes by and this was my reply, I
said you see this road your on is not a one way street, and
this sign you have upon your tree is not that welcoming.

In a Pit?

The trash, the junk, the other stuff, piled upon each other, the slime the muck this stinky stuff, I wish that this was over. I'm sinking deep up to my knees would you help me if you please? This pit I'm in, there's no way out unless someone would pull me out. There are no treasures where I'm at, I stink real badly and that's a fact.

Long behold I see a hand that pulled me out onto the land. I find a river flowing deep, wow I think that this is neat, the flowing fountain is what I need, to wash my body so I feel clean, the fountain flows upon my head, down my chin, and this is what I said, the washing of the water, the cleansing of the soul, no one else can make me whole, but Jesus Christ the savior of us all.

A HARD LESSON LEARNED

It was a nice hot sunshiny day, out in the country
and far away, down in the outback and through
a field, I'm sneaking around and keeping my eyes
peeled, I then get spotted by a herd of cows, they
began to charge me so I run like hell. I'm running as
fast as the speed of sound, the wind is now whistling
like an old hound. I jump the fence and then turn
around just in time to see them skid to the ground.

I walk and walk until at last I come upon a railroad
track. The rails are enticing, they pull me in, I'm now
walking to an unknown land, down the rails I skip
no beat, I'm singing music and strumming a beat,
swallowed up in a one man song, I turn around because
I hear a sound, the sound of a whistle I do believe,
I'm now being chased by a train in the breeze, it's
coming closer as I speed up, trying to find a safe place
to jump, the sides are high with nowhere to go. I'm
running so fast I think I might fall, the train is closer
than ever before, I need to jump before I get hit.

To my right I spot a rope, I take a leap and then
swing out. My hands then slip and I began to fall into a
muddy pit, I'm going under and then pop up, the train
fly's by at the speed of sound, my life was spared and I
almost cried, my heart was pounding on the bank side.
I catch my breath and I'm moving on, as I climb back

up, I'm on my way, I'm now skipping steps on every rail until I come to the end of this trail. I'm walking on and I meet a car recognizing the driver as my grandpa.

He tells me to get up on top; he'll take me home upon his pickup truck. O' boy this is my luck! I'm climbing up on top of the hood, I'm hanging on by the windshield, thinking this will be a trip, grandpa takes off and my hands began to slip, I'm hanging on by a thread, I hope he slows down before I find myself dead. He's going faster than the speed of light, will I live or will I die, as I look up into his face the devil then took his place, he had a grin upon his face, and his eyes were glowing with flames of disgrace.

The road were on is long and wide, paved with lines on both sides, I hope I make it to the end, my grandpa then slowed, as we came to a halt, my legs were shaking and they won't stop, as I climbed down off of the truck my grandpa smiled and gave me a hug, I lived to see another day, my grandpa taught me a lesson that day, never to do what people say, especially when it takes me astray.

Stones and Sticks

Stones and sticks we do it for kicks, the shuffling of an eye. Where we go we do not know, we then are filled with pride. No ancient lips have made this twist, it's rare and it's divine. Sow a seed and reap a harvest that is our specialty. But lying lips is one of the six that cuts just like a knife. Why do we devise these wicked schemes and have detestable eyes?

Innocent blood shall not be shed for it is our life line. Don't rush to evil or you will see your life line sucked right out of thee. Don't walk in step with a false witness who pours out a lie, they have no cares of who they hurt; they only cover up their own dirt. A dissension here, a dissension there, brothers this is wrong, pray that God will give you grace and leave your brother alone.

If I Had My Chance

If I had my chance I'd be the best that I can be. I'd run the race set out for me. I'd be running hard and I wouldn't look back. I'd leave my dust there in the past. I'd run as fast as my legs would go this race I'm running I'm not on my own. I'm reaching for a medal that's shiny and gold. Will I make it to the end well I don't really know? I'll strive for the finish line even if I'm slow.

If I had my chance I'd be the one to show unconditional love no matter what color, size, or strength, let us be what we were made to be living a life without selfishness and greed in hopes of a future of hope and peace. Living to love is what is right not passing judgment but living in the light.

If I had my chance I'd lead a life into victory. I'd be standing on the sidelines pressing in pushing for the one who's in the ring lifting them up and shouting their name refreshing their spirit without any blame hoping they win the final round, and not to get stomped into the ground.

If I had my chance I'd stand up in the face of my enemy not seeking a battle but hoping to win our advisory the devil he has all grins he doesn't care how big that I am his nature is to kill whatever he can I'll stand up and be strong and fight like a man and maybe the devil will run like the wind.

If I had my chance I'd tell what the lord has done for me. I once lived a life that was full of pain longing for the day that god would reign my hopes were crushed, and I'd never be the same until my god reached out his hand and saved me from my ball and chain little did I know the joy to come when he gave me life when I had none.

THE UNJUST MANIPULATIONS

An abuse that sets itself up for game, seeks to destroy those that play. Abuse is a spirit that holds on tight, not caring who it doesn't treat right. Abuse comes in many forms, with that of a mental and then some more. It takes control of your inner thoughts; it tells you your weak when you're not.

That of sexual is one of a kind, it tells you your body is all mine. It forces itself around and about and makes you think you have to give out. It seeks to destroy your purity, and steals your hope and security. It leaves behind only heartache and hurt, and will leave you in poverty and snatch your shirt.

Emotional is one that inflicts with blame, it tells you your dumb and fills you with shame. Anguish rises and egos fall, it's time to tear down that brick wall. Rise up O' weak for your not to blame for the things that others inflict with pain, they speak of things they know nothing about, and tear you down with all those shouts.

Physical pain is by far, the only one that will leave a scar, reminders of years that have long past, violence and abuse and all the attacks. A controlling spirit is its name, not caring who its next victim became; it seeks to destroy like a ravaging wolf, with pride on the outskirts it doesn't let up.

OVERCAME

Dyslexia is by far the most, a unique, technique that makes us coast. Math is hard to comprehend; it makes us fail before we began. Solving problems we cannot do, and sequence is a stumper to.

The letter b or is it d, which ones which, I cannot see, I cannot tell if its dad or bad, this really kind of makes me mab. Why did I have to be born this way? It has caused me trouble all the way.

With dyslexia we can agree, there is a kind of philosophy, which takes us far beyond our self, to tell a story like no one else. Jack wasn't nimble, and Jack wasn't quick, but he sure did jump over that candle stick.

FRIENDS

Friends are a special thing, they build you up
and share there bling, they are not prideful and will
not hurt, and surely they won't drag you through
the dirt. They are there through ups and downs, and
will answer their phones when you're not around.

Friends will get together on a cup of tea, and
talk about the old times when they planted seeds.
Friends don't lie and they sure don't cheat, and
sometimes they will meet you in the street. They'll
shop till they drop just because you're there, so
they can help you find the right underwear.

Friends will laugh when you slip off your
shoe, only because it happens to them to. Don't
worry about the bikini that came off in the lake,
just because they made the same mistake; tie
it in a knot for goodness sake. Friends laugh at
many things only because it is a good thing.

Don't forget about the time in the hotel lobby,
when you were trying to get to the second story,
hoping not to meet anyone you know, you end up in
line headed for a show, noticing all were dressed real
fine, suites and ties O' no it's a wedding line. Dressed
in your swimming suit, this is not good; it's time
to run for cover but you don't know what to do.

What about the walk that was late at night, out on
a golf course friends like to talk, and there to the right
is a man on a bench, sleeping and snoring and startled
us to death, he jumped to this feet and we thought we'd
been had; he was a homeless man who had no bed.

Friends will be there through thick and thin, even
in the times when you need a helping hand. The sauna is
a great place to start, when you're in there sweating and
door gets stuck, this is one time you think you're going to
die, until your friend starts laughing and you want to cry.

How about all those nights getting ready to dance,
zumba is the best thing to work off your abs, were
trying to dance and not giving up, this is aggravating
I hope no one looks. It's time for a break, 30 minutes
to go; a ten gallon drink is sitting on the floor.

Friends are a joy and treasure from the lord;
he gives us that gift to help us soar. He knows
when we stumble that we need a good friend, and
those are who he gave us to help us to the end.

Do what you got to Do

Children are a special gift, the one god gave me
did a trick, I gave her nerds upon her plate, and when
I turned she did not eat. She poked them up into her
nose, all in knowing she could not blow, she pushed
them up unto her eye and now I think I'm going to cry.

A mother's nightmare what do I do? Mothers
panic and fathers are calm, but this is a time I am all
alone. Mothers will do whatever they can, to help the
situation as fast as they can. Mothers will sometimes get
brilliant ideas, just like the one of a vacuum cleaner.

I placed my vacuum upon her nose, in hopes
that the nerd candies are all exposed, red and purple,
white and blue no time to stop there are still a few,
no one knows just how big or small; now I think
I have them all. My mouth is full of nerds and
snot, I could have eaten them but I did not.

Buttercup

My little buttercup is soft and sweet, until she gets mad, then she'll hiss at your feet. If you're not careful she nibbles your toes, as if to say you better let me go. It is now time for her to take a bath, she meows real loud and looks like a drowned rat. Bath time is over roll her up in a towel, blow dry her hair and put her by the door.

Every morning at 6 a.m she sounds her alarm and tries to get in, she's ready to greet whoever comes out, in hopes that somebody will set her breakfast out, she'll lick your arm she'll lick your leg whichever one gets in her way. She likes to run, she likes to play, she likes to jump up and grab your leg.

She sometimes goes unto the vet, and she doesn't like it, not one little bit, she gets some shots, and she gets wormed. I hope she's ready to return. God he gives us all good things, and tells us to take care of them. Be sure you know the condition of your cat, and every animal after that.

Jennifer Miller

EASTER

Chariots of fire, flowers in bloom do they go together, well I don't presume. God is amazing in all he does; his grace is around us in what he done. Jesus died on the cross to erase our sins and on the third day he rose again, if that isn't enough to get your heart beating then think about the times he did all the healings, miraculous yes, luck no, he never puts on a show, he is the real thing and I hope that you know he did it for me and he did it for you, to show us the way that we are to go. Easter time is a special thing, if you never gave your heart to the only king, now is the time you can be set free.

Rise up Saints

Fear is a chain that holds on fast, it won't let you go and it wears a mask. It tries to hide and it won't make a sound, should I keep it or let it go, this is a story that I think you know, it hides in the gutters it lurks in the streets, it says you're incompetent and incomplete. It takes you down a road you don't want to go and leaves you abandoned with no home.

Fear is a discrepancy against the truth; it tries to hold you back and keeps you in a noose, it won't let you be what you were meant to be, you try to find deliverance but it won't set you free, freedom is a gift from the one and only king, just as when Daniel stood before Nebuchadnezzar, he thought for sure that his life was over, and all because he stood up for what was right, god sent an angel in the form of a man, who brought deliverance unto their land.

Daniel was a man inspiring and true, he interpreted dreams and came to the rescue. Nebuchadnezzar was full of pride he oppressed the weak until they cried, his power was taken until he seen that god is the one who made him king. The writing on the wall, yes indeed it was to proclaim the end of his creed.

Daniel was a man noble and true, he was thrown into a lion's den, but he got rescued, he wasn't afraid to do what was right, he never got a scratch or even a bite. God

Jennifer Miller

lifted him up and gave him a robe, to show all people that He sits on the throne, god lives forever and his dominion never ends, now is the time to give your heart to him.

When kingdoms rise against the saints, the lion sneaks about and tries to intimidate. The eagle is one who seeks you out, and then accuses you without a doubt. The bear likes to fight and put up a front, he has long claws and teeth that can crush, but god is bigger than all that stuff.

The leopard is pretty and stands at great heights, he tries to deceive the world as a whole, but god knows he only puts on a show. The fourth one is different than all the rest he seems to have power to trample our zest, he is hard hearted and acts on his own, he doesn't have the spirit while he sits on his throne.

Then comes the one with a voice so strong, he speaks with arrogance and a heart of stone, but he doesn't remain upon his throne, as the wind it blows upon our hearts, Jesus comes all clothed in white, he sits upon his blazing throne, to tell you yes, you will stand alone, the book of life he will then hold, and pronounce the guilty and all that is wrong.

The ram and the goat what a nasty combination, raging fits and a bad intervention, goats will rise to greater powers while training there young to take over the nations. Rebellion and witchcraft are one in the same, setting itself up to trample the saints, tearing down the sanctuaries and living in vain.

Confession of sin, our nation does need, the time of restoration and a decree, but first reconstruction before our king, the lord Jesus Christ glowing with a beam, will stand before a man highly esteemed, wars are raging and armies fighting and flattery will deceive, but those who live a righteous life will not be deceived. Riches and treasures will rise to the top but only for a time. God will destroy the one who lifts himself up in vain.

Michael will come when the distress is great, and rise to protect the saints, all who are wise will then shine and there name will be in the book, but those who are not will be condemned and will not be over looked, all will rise from among the grave, some to life and some to shame, now is not the time to live your life in vain.

Passing Judgment

When you know that you know that you know
you're doing right, all the passing judgments will be
done in spite. When god is on our side then it will be
alright, so don't live your life worrying about a fight.
God is our hope and god is our peace he won't leave
you hanging there by your hands and your feet.

All the looks and all the stares from all those people
who don't really care, it should give you a desire to push
on through, strength and a shield for the battles to
come, surrounded by the enemy and a heart of love.

Next time you pass judgment on things unknown,
take a look in the mirror and see what you've done
wrong, it might just be that the finger you point
will come back around and bite you in the butt.

Second Mother

What can surpass a mother's love, when she lives
or when she gives hugs, something down deep she
cannot hide, a nurturing spirit that is inside. Through
all the hurts and scraped up knees, through all the
troubles and every need, she is a woman of integrity.

She stands in the gap for the ones without a
mother, giving out hugs and inviting them over,
she understands their needs and loves like no
other. Who can be patient who can be strong? She
gives chocolate milk to the one who had none.

Blessing others is what she lives for, setting
up Easter eggs to color and more, little does
she know they never done that before, feeling a
warmth of the spirit grow, watching the smiles
fill their face, as she fills up on god's grace.

It does bring joy, it does bring peace, to give to
others the things they need, a mother can't hide the
love in her heart, especially when god says that this is
right. When they grow up they will always remember,
all the fun times, and when they came over, and
they might even call you their second mother.

STENCH IN THE AIR

The stench of pig pooh that fills the air, burning my nose hairs as I gasp and stair, a lisp in a lip he has gone astray, will he come back my heart is in dismay. He walks around without a care in the world, not realizing his smell has been discovered, it's obvious to everyone except this odd fellow that god is not the source of this life that is shallow.

Twiddle Dee Dee twiddle Dee dumb, he's wasted his life on spinach and rum, sauerkraut and rhubarb, cantaloupe and more, this is not the life god created him for. A ho and a hum a biting of the nail, he's now filled with nervousness and no direction to spare. He lost all connection with the creator of life, will he come back? Well he better decide.

There in the distance the father did see the periodical son that had left with greed, he then returned home with a very desperate need. The father then took him and washed his clothes, butchered the calf and said come on. The party then started as they began to celebrate, for the son who was lost and then god saved.

GOD LIKE

With a God like faith we can conquer the world, but what about our taste will we over indulge? Food is for the body and we're made to enjoy, but know when to stop or your faith will be destroyed. Food is very good and dessert is even better, it fuels the body and makes us strong, but don't over eat or you'll turn into a time bomb.

With a God like faith we can conquer the world, but how about our touch and the things we do, do we pray for others needs as we are suppose to? Touch can mean several things, can you feel or do you sting? Feeling goes deep as to help others needs. A sting is wound that should not be.

With a God like faith we can conquer the world, but where is our focus when it comes to the truth? Our eyes are a window unto the soul, it is showing others who we are. Be careful O' eyes what you see, are they darkened or are they light? Don't let temptation be your guide, your eyes will go dim and there'll be no sight, keep your focus on the things that are right.

With a God like faith we can conquer the world, but when the smell of death lays at our feet we wonder where our life has went. The fragrance of death or the fragrance of life, only Christ has the power to rise, he is a sweet smelling aroma for all to enjoy, draw near to him and you won't be sorry.

Jennifer Miller

With a God like faith we can conquer the world, our hearing is a special part, that can make our faith grow, and faith that grows from hearing can make us strong, unless of course were unyielding and numb. Let our ears be open and hearts be loosed, so we don't miss the blessings of gods gracious truth.

It is God who is the author and perfecter of our faith; it is God who gave us all of these things. It is God who knows our every need. It is God who opens our eyes to see. It is God who knows us all by name. It is God in heaven who doesn't change.

Strength on the Inside

My arms maybe little without much strength, and others may laugh at what they see. People may not think I can carry a load, but that is just not simply so. I do not have to prove a thing, because God is the Lord who has made me king, kings don't stoop to a level that's dull, and don't have to prove that there king at all.

Laugh as you will merchants of death, you've opened the door to Satan's breath, your laugh is creepy and your smile deceiving, the window to your heart is a little revealing. I will not falter I will not faint; I will stand strong upon my faith. No temptation has seized me that I can't remain, steady and strong in the face of a storm, no I will not show you the strength of my arm, leave your package and be on your way, mission accomplished and not in vain.

My name is imbedded on the finger of God; he knows me well and has given me life. I'm not who I was when I gave him my heart, the things I use to hate, I now have a love. His words are impressed upon my heart, to show me the way to live my life right. My strength doesn't come from what you can see, but my strength is hidden on the inside of me.

Jennifer Miller

THE RIGHT KEY

Standing at the entrance with a ticket in hand, hoping to see some animals upon this land. It's not what I expected when I looked to my right; there at the spinning gate with a boy by his side, was a little rebel who tried to hide. He got himself locked on the other side, his friend tried to help him and got caught to, me to the rescue but what do I do? I frantically look for an open door, but all are locked let's look some more.

Walking over to the other side, the boys are scared and want to cry, I need a keeper with a key, to unlock the door and set them free. I shake the door and it breaks loose, 20 minutes later they come out of their noose. Laughing and jumping they've been set free, their no longer on the outside, they live in victory.

This book shall now come to a close, I want to thank you for reading and I hope your faith grows. Like a flower that springs up for a day, we live and breathe and then fade away.

Blessings to you and all that is yours, may God grant you peace and your hope be restored. May healing take place upon your soul and transformation bloom a heart of gold.